Nick Williams had a very successful conventional sales career but wasn't happy and fulfilled, so he found the courage to leave and follow his heart to find out what he would love to do with his life. This eventually led him to work as a Director of Alternatives at St James's – a premier venue in London for major authors and workshop leaders from around the world. Nick is also the Founder of the Heart at Work project. He is an internationally established workshop presenter, works in mainline business as a consultant and trainer for the public and private sectors and is an expert in personal coaching. He has been widely featured in the media as a leading authority on the world of work and how our work can be an expression of the best in us – our heart and soul. His work has helped such diverse groups as lawyers, teachers, managing directors, trainers, doctors, the clergy, social workers, the self-employed and the unemployed.

THE 12 PRINCIPLES OF THE WORK WE WERE BORN TO DO

NICK WILLIAMS

Thorsons

Thorsons
An Imprint of HarperCollins*Publishers*
77–85 Fulham Palace Road,
Hammersmith, London W6 8JB

The Thorsons website address is:
www.thorsons.com

and *Thorsons*
are trademarks of
HarperCollins*Publishers* Limited

First published by Thorsons 2002

1 3 5 7 9 10 8 6 4 2

© Nick Williams 1999, 2002

The text of *The 12 Principles of the Work We Were Born To Do*
has been extracted from *The Work We Were Born To Do*

Nick Williams asserts the moral right to
be identified as the author of this work

A catalogue record of this book
is available from the British Library

ISBN 0 00 713853 9

Printed and bound in Great Britain by
Clays Ltd, St. Ives plc

Contents

Introduction

Within the pages of this book you will find the beginnings of a transformed way of working – the work we were born to do. The work we were born to do offers each one of us personal fulfillment and a way to express our full potential. It is based around 12 simple principles. Those principles are explored in this book, which will help you to do two things:

1 Identify and root out any unhelpful ideas or thoughts about work.
2 Sow useful and supportive thoughts to enhance the quality of your working life.

Thoughts are like seeds – we often accept them unquestioningly and plant them in the fertile soil of our minds, and then live our lives according to them. We reap a daily harvest and, depending on what we sowed originally, the result is either a life based on expressing our sense of self-worth, love, creativity, abundance and possibility, or a life choked by scarcity, fear, worry and struggle.

Thoughts and beliefs are first cause: we can only see what we believe; that is the way our minds work. This means that the quality of our working experience is determined by the quality of our thoughts about our lives and ourselves: they are one and the same. That's why, if we want to create any change in our life experiences, we first need to change our inner worlds.

Some of our negative thoughts may seem so deeply ingrained that they feel unchangeable. But with time, intention and repetition we can all change our thinking, as our thoughts are the only things that we really do have dominion over.

In this book you will find easy exercises, meditations, transforming thoughts and affirmations designed to help you overcome any unhelpful conditioning and tap into the unlimited resources of your deeper mind and spirit. In these straightforward techniques lie the seeds of the work you were born to do.

Principle 1

DEFINING THE WORK
WE WERE BORN TO DO

We are all unique and precious. And, whether we realize it or not, we all have talents and gifts. Our first task is to discover these gifts, which we will do by finding and following whatever gives us joy. As we do so, we will discover a reservoir of energy within us. We will begin to create our own niche in life, which will lie in whatever comes naturally to us. We may need to face and shed old self-concepts and doubt. The work we were born to do leads us to find previously untapped strength of will and inner power flowing from our own spirit.

Everyone has been called for some particular work, and the desire for that work has been put in his or her heart.

JALALUDDIN RUMI,
12th-century Persian mystic and poet

True work is not a job that we do to make a living, survive and pay the bills. True work is concerned with finding and expressing the best within us – our love, creativity, heart and spirit – whilst creating the money we need to pay the bills and to live our lives as a by-product. This is the work we were born to do: it is about following our inner voice, heeding the spiritual call and living our purpose by finding what is great in us and letting it out. It is about having a passion for something, then deciding and committing to putting all our love, energy and creativity into fulfilling it. It may not just be about doing something different; it also involves discovering a new and more authentic way of being in the world and living our own lives. Within each of us is the power to create rewarding and fulfilling work, and inside us lie the power and resources we need to do it.

EXERCISE

Here are some questions to help you begin to find the work you were born to do:

♦ Where is your joy? Where is your passion and motivation? What makes you feel most energized?

♦ What experiences, throughout the whole of your working life, have you found most rewarding, inspiring, touching or meaningful?

♦ What work would you love to do if you had all the money and time you needed already, or if all the work paid the same?

◆ Who would you love to work with?

◆ What would you love to be doing and giving? For whom?

◆ And what would you receive from that, both materially and non-materially?

LISTENING TO OURSELVES AGAIN

The answers to the work we were born to do will not be found outside in the busyness of our daily activities; we will find them when we take the time to listen to our intuition, to notice our feelings and to be with our being. We can do this in any quiet place, such as a room in our home, somewhere in nature or a church or a park. This means finding sanctuary space. However, the place itself doesn't even matter that much, because sanctuary is an intention and an attitude rather than a physical place. With practice we can create sanctuary space in more and more situations, although we may need to start with a physical place of peace and calm.

Sanctuary space will help us to tune into our inner direction and divine guidance. It will help us to let our own hearts be the greatest influence in our lives, as we turn away from the voices of doubt and fear in our own minds and the opinions of others seeking to influence us.

Affirmation

'There is some work that I was born to do; I can discover it by following my heart, my joy and my God-given creative gifts.'

INTENTION AND ATTENTION

The possibilities for the work we were born to do exist right now, yet they may lie just outside our current perception.

Whatever we focus on, think about or worship, expands; through our own consciousness we create lack or plenty, pain or joy, purpose or struggle. We are what we think about. That is why a large part of the work we were born to do is concerned with choosing to place our attention on different things and to establish our intention. This discipline alone can positively transform our experience of work. We'll learn to look for opportunities rather than problems, creativity rather than boredom, inner power rather than outer limitations.

When we have our attention in the present and our intention for the future, we are at our most powerful, because as we set our intentions for the direction of our life we begin to set in place synchronistic events that support us. Our intention sends out ripples and stimulates possible ways of bringing that intention to fruition.

EXERCISE

♦ Formulate a list of your deepest and most inspiring desires and intentions. Look at them several times a day – pay attention to them – and remind yourself of what they mean to you. Remind yourself early in the morning, last thing at night and before silence and meditation.

♦ Remove the limits and allow yourself to dream about possibilities, the kind of work that would really inspire you, with no thought at all for *how* you might create it.

♦ Release *emotional attachment* to the outcome of your thoughts and intentions. The organizing intelligence that runs the whole of creation will work with your intentions too.

♦ Live in and accept the present moment as fully as possible, knowing that you are creating and directing your working life in each moment of your life.

♦ Notice the ways in which your intentions are being fulfilled.

> ### Meditation
>
> 'I am willing to listen to my inner thoughts, feelings and atti-
> tudes, and to find the answers within rather than seek
> answers outside. I am willing to trust myself again. I simply
> ask that I rediscover my sense of inspiration and aliveness,
> my passion, joy and enthusiasm.'

CELEBRATING OUR TALENTS

The work we were born to do may require effort, but not struggle. It doesn't mean being good at everything, just some things;
fish swim beautifully and naturally, but don't walk so well; cats
make great companions but can't cook; babies are good at
being babies, but not nuclear physicists.

EXERCISE

- What is your response to the idea of being talented and
  gifted? Do you feel excitement and interest, or fear and
  resistance?

- What, in your mind, are your strengths, talents and gifts?

- What have you been told your strengths are?

- How did you feel when you were told? Did you believe it?

- Pick four significant people in your life, such as a partner,
  boss, colleague or parent. In your mind, ask, 'What do I
  think each one would perceive to be my strengths?' Ask
  yourself and hear what answers come to you. When you feel
  up to it, go and ask those people to tell you. Listen, and take
  note of what they say. How do their answers match your
  own feelings?

Start to value more what comes naturally and easily to you, as to have your gifts go unexpressed is one of the most terrible forms of poverty. The work we were born to do is about celebrating our individual abilities and choices, based on our individual inner and outer needs, and it is unique for each of us. What singles us out as being different may be the rare thing we possess. It is the special thing that gives each of us our worth, and yet that's just what we often try to suppress.

Transforming Thought
Who you are is the greatest gift of all.

CREATING OUR NICHE

Finding a niche for ourselves means valuing our idiosyncrasies, our quirkiness, even our moods – which may just be our greatest gift. Ultimately nobody else can compete with us for our niche, because only we can fill it in our unique way. Finding our niche means discovering exactly where we belong, and being in our element. It may be that our niche has been created by someone else but fits us well, or we may create it ourselves from our own sense of inner vision and by understanding how to use our own creative powers. When we find our niche, the money will come as a beautiful by-product. More importantly, we will discover that:

♦ our inner and outer worlds become more integrated and balanced

♦ we can be more of our natural shape, our natural selves

♦ work and pleasure are unified

♦ we feel recognized

- we feel safe and that we belong
- we are in alignment with ourselves, and have integrity
- we are on track and on purpose
- we support the spiritual side of ourselves in work
- the reward of our work is the joy of doing it, not only the approval of others or external rewards

In terms of the work we were born to do our niche could be:

- part time or full time
- self-employed or employed, or a combination
- a portfolio career or one main career
- a small part of our life or a major part of our life

We may even have to create our niche; it may not exist yet.

Transforming Thought

Your greatest desire is not just to *have* more, but to *be* more of who you are.

WHAT NEEDS TO HAPPEN BEFORE YOU'LL MAKE A CHANGE?

What are you waiting for? Do you think you need permission or encouragement from someone outside you before you can change or uncover your niche? What permission would someone else give you? Give that permission to yourself.

Four Simple Ways to Implement Principle 1

* Choose to do what you love, or do more often what you enjoy in the way you love.

* Notice what you most enjoy about today.

* Ask yourself what would be really inspiring for you, and do something about it.

* Value your uniqueness.

Principle 2

UNDOING OUR CONDITIONING

We have stifled our natural self and our spirit through the conditioning that we have absorbed throughout our lives. Our conditioning comprises the beliefs, attitudes and opinions that others have invited us to take on, which we may have mistaken for facts. We are called to identify, examine and discard beliefs that are not useful and are not true for us, and to continue the emotional healing that is required.

Even in the best of circumstances, we are all just learning. No parents are fully enlightened. Children will unconsciously absorb their parents' fears and biases and later in life, one hopes, learn to become conscious of these conditioned attitudes and find ways to release them. This is normal; this is the work we all have to do.

RICHARD MOSS,
author and teacher

Our beliefs and our conditioning determine how we see the world. The working life we have created *is* the manifestation of our beliefs; by exploring our beliefs and undoing our conditioning, we will open ourselves to the work we were born to do.

To start the process of change we must understand our current position and what has brought us here. We don't sit down one day and decide what we are going to believe, but we can make decisions based upon the thousands of influences and messages that we have received every day of our life from everyone around us. Our beliefs are largely unconscious and are like glass walls – we don't see them and only know they are there when we bump into them. But to get past them, we first have to know they are there.

The following exercise will bring into your awareness some of the major beliefs that you have developed in your life, specifically around work. Some of these beliefs will support you in creating the work you were born to do, whilst others will squash your spirit and inspiration.

EXERCISE

Cast your mind back to when you were younger and think about the kinds of messages you got about work – both helpful and unhelpful – from people and organizations such as:

- ◆ your family – parents, guardians, siblings and relatives
- ◆ your school, teachers or careers advisors
- ◆ professional bodies
- ◆ the media
- ◆ peers and colleagues
- ◆ religious and political leaders

Don't censure them or judge them; simply be aware and make a note of them.

Transforming Thought

You created your own belief system; you have the power within you to change it too.

To change the future, we need to change our perception of our past. The most important aspect of learning is to unlearn our erroneous thinking, including the top ten spirit-squashing beliefs held by most of us.

1 Our purpose in work is to get approval and acceptance

We often place more importance on what others think of us than on what we think of ourselves. We need to discover what we truly want in our own hearts as opposed to what we want because it will win us the approval of others.

2 Everything good is outside us

We have been taught that everything good is outside us and needs to be worked hard for. This has blinded us to the fact that each of us already contains all that we are looking for, because our *unconditioned self* is whole and complete, with or without external status symbols, and completely abundant.

3 Work is hard, a struggle, even a punishment

We often believe we are here to suffer. The work we were born to do is based on changing this core belief, so that our work is no longer a punishment but a way of expressing our true creative goodness.

4 Work must involve sacrifice

Sacrifice is the belief in self-denial, and the idea that it will buy us something of value like love and approval or a place in heaven. The work we were born to do demands no sacrifice, offering instead the choice to relinquish old and unhelpful beliefs.

5 We live in a state of non-participating consciousness

We have been conditioned to believe that we are separate from our environment, from each other and from the creative force behind all life. Yet the deeper truth is that the world responds to us, is part of us, and we are part of it.

6 Work is 9 to 5, five days a week, 48 weeks a year, for most of our life

This is what we have been taught a 'proper' job entails. Our expectations of work are generally so low that perhaps we need to invent a new word for joyful, loving, spontaneous, creative work. Our work could be creative and have many strands to it.

7 We create what we want by studying and eliminating what we don't want

We've become fascinated by what we *don't* want. Yet when we nurture what we *do* want and pay attention to it, we create more of it. We believe we learn through mistakes and pain, not joy and success.

8 Our work defines who we are

Many of us equate what we do for a living and what we earn with who we are and how valuable we are. So if we are not defined by a job, our whole sense of identity, self-esteem and self-confidence may be threatened. But we are valuable whether we work or not. We are valuable simply because we exist.

9 There isn't enough – scarcity rules

Our whole world is fuelled by the belief that there isn't enough of anything to go round. This sense of lack keeps us from focusing on the here and now, which is potentially laden with all the gifts and possibilities we could ever want.

10 Money and financial survival are the major purposes of work

We may believe that the goal of work lies in financial security. Work becomes a 'necessary evil' in order to survive. However, although we may have to work, we can choose *how* we do it as well as *what* we do. We can give ourselves joyfully to our work, whatever it is.

Transforming Thought

What you can do easily and naturally is also very valuable.

UNDOING OUR CONDITIONING

There are two attitudes to dealing with the emotional patterns created by our conditioning: we can use them either to feel like a victim by passing the blame on to everyone else, or to heal ourselves. We don't have to re-create ourselves, but simply unlearn all that isn't true about us.

Meditation

'I ask for the power to see beyond my conditioning – to realize that I am not the limitations that I have come to believe I am. I ask for guidance in releasing the limits to my love, my creativity, my joy, my peace and passion, my inspiration and vision.'

EXERCISE

To change anything you need first to be aware of it and to accept how it is. Then you can take the following steps.

♦ Decide what you would *like* to be true, and begin to focus your thoughts on it. This process may take time as you shift energy from your old beliefs to your new ideal.

♦ Begin to liberate yourself from wounding beliefs, such as 'I'm no good' or 'I must suffer'. These beliefs may go so deep that you may feel that you can never change them, but you can free yourself, layer by layer, perhaps through some form of daily practice such as repeating an affirmation.

♦ Develop a witness stance to all your thoughts, including your beliefs: try to take a step back and observe them, commenting on them to yourself. Through developing the witness position, you will come to realize that you are not your beliefs or your feelings, but the whole person who experiences them.

Affirmation

'I am willing to accept the truth about myself, however wonderful and splendid that may be.'

VISION – CREATING A NEW FUTURE

If we don't change our beliefs about ourselves, about our gifts and talents and our possibilities for work, our life becomes just more of the same. Instead of living ten thousand different days, we live the same day ten thousand times. We want a new day to dawn. We can develop a vision for ourselves and our working life, one which will be new, exciting and inspiring, which will make us want to get out of bed in the morning and work. We can ignite ourselves and set our hearts on fire again.

EXERCISE

- Do you believe it is *at all* possible for anyone to be really happy in work? If you don't, do some research and meet some of the thousands of people who do enjoy their work.

- Do you believe it is possible for *you* to be happy in work? If not, write down why.

- What would you *need to believe* to create the next step in the work you were born to do?

When we begin to understand that our mind is the starting point for all we see and experience we move on to genuine empowerment. Our goal is to change our own conditioning and the way we think about the world, as much as it is to change the world itself. The key lies not in the nature of the work itself, but in the attitude and spirit with which we approach it.

Four Simple Ways to Implement Principle 2

* Spend your energy today believing, 'Who I am and what I do are really important', and notice how your day goes.

* Write down some of your old beliefs and burn the note; then write out a new list for yourself.

* Try to visualize an old belief in your mind: give it a character, then see it disappear as you embrace a new one in its place.

* Actively seek out someone who is passionate about their work. Discover what their beliefs are.

Principle 3

EXPLORING THE
SPIRIT OF OUR WORK

What is most important is not the work that we do but the attitude and consciousness with which we do it. We can learn to transform our consciousness gradually from fear, lack and need to love, abundance and creativity. We are on an adventure of transforming our attitude and consciousness, and as we return to the awareness that we are spirit and that the basis of life is consciousness we begin to transcend our current limitations.

Everything you see has its roots in the unseen world, the forms may change yet the essence remains the same. Every wonderful sight will vanish, every sweet word will fade but do not be disheartened, the source they come from is eternal, growing, branching out, giving new life and new joy. Why do you weep? The source is within you and this whole cosmos is springing up from it.

JALALUDDIN RUMI,
12th-century Persian mystic and poet

The spirit of our work refers to two ideas: firstly, that in essence we *are* spirit and there are no limits to our creative ability; and, secondly, that our inner spirit is manifested by the attitude and state of mind with which we work.

For many, the very mention of 'spirit' has them running away for fear of religious dogma, rules and guilt. Yet, in the simplest possible terms, spirit is our own nature. A core idea at the heart of the work we were born to do, which may overthrow much of what we have been led to believe, is that behind the entire physical world as we know it is *non-physical substance* and that behind all appearances of physical reality is something essential that is *non-physical*. True prosperity is not what we make or collect, but the degree to which we are in the flow of this non-physical essence and willing to be a channel through which it can flow.

NURTURING OUR AWARENESS OF SPIRIT

We don't have to nurture and strengthen spirit itself – it is already there, strong and indestructible. What we do need to do is strengthen our *awareness* of spirit. As we do that we become strengthened by it.

Here are some practical ways to strengthen your awareness of spirit in your daily life:

1　Take time to be in awe of the intelligence behind all the appearances of life

Get awe-struck by the number of galaxies and stars there are in the universe, the sheer size of it. Marvel at the force that maintains and co-ordinates nature.

2　Take time in quiet and solitude

Listen to the silence in your mind. In that silence answers will come to you, as it is pregnant with ideas and universal knowledge. Recognize your own wisdom.

3　Notice the thinker of your thoughts

When you have a thought, stop and ask, 'Who is thinking it?' This is the silent witness, your own spirit.

4　Remember that behind all appearances is essence

Remind yourself that everything you see in the physical world had its origin in the non-physical world, in thought and essence.

5　Mindfulness

Mindfulness is concerned with simply living in *this present*. It sounds so simple, but it is probably the most difficult thing for us to do.

Transforming Thought

Who you are in essence is an eternal spirit; you can become more and more aware of this.

AWAKENING THE ESSENCE OR SPIRIT WITH WHICH WE APPROACH OUR WORK

Happiness and meaning in our work come not from any particular job, any one achievement or any amount of money, but from the spirit in which we do it. This can be such a challenging idea for us, because we are generally so attached to thinking that *physical* things, conditions and circumstances will make us happy. True success is more often concerned with a change of consciousness than a change of circumstances.

The key to the work we were born to do is that we *can* change our attitude, our state of mind, our motivation, even the consciousness with which we work. We *can* make the transition from working with resentment, boredom or dissatisfaction to working with gratitude, pleasure and happiness. In doing so we can see our existing work differently, and even begin to transform it, as well as begin to see new possibilities that we hadn't seen before.

Meditation

'Let me discover more of who I truly am. I wish for the guidance that will help me to discover my spirit and its relation to the spirit behind all things. I am willing to discover how my happiness will come not from any particular work, but from the spirit in which I work.'

EXERCISE

Ask yourself the following questions:

♦ How could I change the spirit in which I work right now? How could I change my attitude so that it would lighten the atmosphere in which I work?

♦ What do I really want my work to be about, beyond what I

actually do? What qualities and experiences do I want to be at the heart of my work?

♦ What do I want it to be a vehicle for, other than making money?

♦ What do I want the essence and spirit of my work to be?

Affirmation

The qualities you have identified as being important to you are already inside you, and the best way of drawing them out is to use the affirmation 'I AM'.

Once we have got clear around the essence, we see how we can create a vehicle or structure for this essence to flow through.

THE VEHICLE OF OUR WORK

Sometimes we are so caught in old and limiting ways of seeing work that we find it a challenge even to think of work being qualitatively different to what it is now.

EXERCISE

♦ What is missing from your work now, or has been from previous employment? Write down all that is missing, and turn this around into a sentence that starts, 'What I want to create and experience in my work is . . .'

♦ Could you do what you are doing now in a way that you would enjoy more, that would support or inspire you more? Could you change the spirit of what you do? What qualities do you most want to experience in your working life? Joy, connection, aliveness, hope, vision, abundance, love, growth, inspiration?

♦ Pick five positive words that you would normally be *least* likely to associate with work: for example, joyful, exciting, free, sensual, inspiring, beautiful ... Be really free with the words! Now take these five words and turn them into a positive sentence, starting 'My work is/gives me/allows me ...'

We are not looking for perfection here, simply a change of direction. Our heart knows the essence of our life's work – it is up to us to rediscover our spirit, to decide what form we want that essence to take and to create appropriate ways of working that suit our spirit.

Transforming Thought

You can discover or create a way of working that is big enough for your spirit.

Below are some of the ways you can bring this essence into being:

♦ Realize and know that essence is already within you, *in your very being*. It just needs to be drawn forth, so be these qualities.

♦ Give essence your attention. Notice where creativity and love already exist: look for them, seek them out and choose to create them. Don't complain or hate – create!

♦ Give essence your intention. Focus on it, make it your desire, determine it and choose it. Remember that what you pay attention to expands.

◆ Visualize and meditate on the qualities that you want to characterize the essence of your work. Form a relationship with them, make friends with them, and study them.

◆ Detach from the outcome.

The essence of our work is not just about the job of work we do, but about the *kind* of doctor, teacher, manager, trainer or musician we want to be. It may not be *what* we do that we want to change, but *the spirit in which we do it*: we may want to be a different kind of doctor, salesman, teacher, consultant or shop assistant. All work can be healing in the broadest sense. With love, kindness, humour and caring, we can make any work uplifting and raise spirits.

Allow your spirit to touch the lives of others. Extend your kindness and generosity by showing others just how much you appreciate them. Let your spirit go to work.

Three Simple Ways to Implement Principle 3

* Do more often what you love, enjoy and like.

* Throw yourself into your work enthusiastically without concerning yourself with the outcome.

* Take a piece of paper and write down the names of six significant people in your work. Drop them a note telling them of your gratitude to them.

Principle 4

AWAKENING THE HEART AT WORK

Our feeling heart is our guide and compass, showing our true path through joy and our false paths through pain and suffering. It is our guide to love, and we can learn to bring our love and compassion into any work we do, or to create new work from the inspiration of our heart. Our heart knows while our head supposes and throws up doubt after doubt; we can rely on our heart.

Buddha always emphasized a balance of wisdom and compassion: a good brain and a good heart should work together ... These two must be developed in balance, and when they are, the result is material progress accompanied by good spiritual development. Heart and mind working in harmony will yield a truly peaceful and friendly human family.

One of our biggest struggles occurs when our heart is not in our work; in short, when we don't do what we love or don't love what we do. What moves and touches the heart is what makes us human, and when we don't engage our heart we are likely to be just going through the motions. Our heart is vital to us in many senses, and seems to have a mind of its own. We are often experts at focusing on what we don't want in our lives, and so it is to our heart that we should turn to discover what we really do want. We can use our head in service of our heart, for our head can only *suppose*, while our heart *knows*.

The more we are able to listen to our hearts, and are able to love and be happy with ourselves as well as others, the more we will be able to love what we do. If we find it hard to love ourselves, we will find it hard to be satisfied with whatever we create or achieve. Remember, we were all born to love and be loved, and in essence loving is the work we were born to do.

Meditation

'I wish to be healed of the mad belief that I will be most secure doing what I dislike or hate. I ask for the power to be healed of the belief that I need to sacrifice myself. I want to experience how my happiness in my work is a gift and inspiration to others as well as myself.'

THE LANGUAGE OF OUR HEART

Let's be clear about one thing – our heart will never tell us what we *should*, *ought to* or *must* do; those are the commands of our ego. Our heart will simply show us how to be true to ourselves, our own nature. Here are some ways that our heart communicates to us:

♦ through words

♦ through feelings and sensations

♦ through dreams or symbols

Intuition is the language of the soul speaking through the heart. Our intuition may not make *logical* sense, but it makes heartfelt sense, and sense to our need to be whole and have integrity. Intuition, rather than logic, is often the way we break out of old struggles, mind-sets and limitations.

EXERCISE

♦ When have you felt most intuitive, guided and inspired in your life? What events, situations and circumstances were present?

♦ What would you do in your life if you knew that you would be guided in each moment to say or do the most appropriate thing? How do you feel about that level of trust and confidence?

♦ Simply listen out for your intuition. What is the quiet voice behind all the loud voices telling you to be or do? Thank that voice and offer to build a stronger and stronger relationship with it.

Transforming Thought

Your heart is your true north, your compass of love and integrity in your work.

WHAT IS YOUR HEART IN?

Largely we've come to believe that our heart, and our deeper emotions, *shouldn't* be involved in our work. Of course, some boundaries are important, but the connection with the heart makes all the difference when discovering the work we were born to do. We need to free the heart and build up our enthusiasm, excitement, love and inspiration.

EXERCISE

♦ Keep noticing what you enjoy and love; make it the object of your attention. Write what you notice in a journal. Remember that what we pay attention to grows and expands.

♦ If you still aren't clear what you love and enjoy, or don't have an unfulfilled dream, notice what you *could* love and *could* enjoy, or other people's ideas that touch you.

♦ If the voice of 'But how could you ever do that or make a living out of that?' comes up, say, 'Thank you for sharing; we'll come back to that question.' If we don't get excited enough about ideas, every problem can seem insurmountable, but when we set our heart on an idea, we will discover the ways *how* as we go.

PUTTING YOUR HEART
INTO YOUR WORK RIGHT NOW

We all need to know that people care. We can nourish each other and ourselves through small and large acts of love and kindness every day. When we are caring in our work we will inspire others to care in their work. We will help our colleagues and ourselves to work from the heart.

Transforming Thought

You can get more deeply in touch with your heart by choosing gratitude.

A great starting point is to make the most of our present situation by being kind to our colleagues and learning to love what we do now. We have already discovered the key ingredient in loving our work is not what we do, but the spirit and attitude with which we do it. So try to be as happy as possible with yourself, with others, with your work and with life right now. Once you can do this, you will find it easier to explore new ways of working from the heart.

EXERCISE

♦ What in your work, and outside it, gives you the most joy and pleasure at the moment?

♦ Think back to all the work and jobs you have ever done and remember the parts, even if they were small, that you most enjoyed and found most rewarding. What people, circumstances or attitudes were present there and then?

♦ At what times in your life have you felt your heart was most open?

♦ When can you remember being told that *your* kindness touched somebody else?

♦ Who do you know, or could you know, who could be a mentor, helping, guiding and encouraging you to find and follow what you love?

♦ If you were to be an inspiration to yourself, what would you have been, become or achieved?

♦ What would make you venture your heart again in your work now?

♦ If you worked for love, not money, what would you love to do?

♦ When you think of doing what you love, what are the first thoughts that come to your mind? For example: '... and I'll starve' or '... and I'll be really happy' or '... and people will be jealous'. Write down six immediate responses. Interestingly, many people go a little blank when they think about this – maybe you did – because we actually have precious little conception of what would happen. Take time to think about what you think might happen, and what you would like to happen. This will help flush out some of your fantasies, both helpful and unhelpful.

Many people are now being forced to review the belief that work is a duty with little place for joy, as they discover that they are no longer secure doing a job they don't enjoy. The old contract with employers of 'We buy your loyalty, and get you to do what you don't necessarily enjoy, but we'll look after you' is rapidly disappearing, so we've started to think along the lines of 'If an employer is not going to take care of me, I'll start taking care of myself.'

Affirmation

'I am creating the work I love by listening to and following my heart.'

We *can* create what we love, but first we have to discover what it is we love. Finding our heart in our work requires us to make a shift in thinking from what we could do and what others want us to do, to what we want to do. And to view money as an incidental benefit to doing what we love in our life is the most blessed of all experiences, as we will explore in Principle 5.

Three Simple Ways to Implement Principle 4

* Do something for your boss to make him or her feel valued and appreciated.

* Find something special and precious to celebrate.

* Get your team together and pose the question to everyone, 'How can we work together in ways that are more fun, supportive, inspiring and loving?' Brainstorm the answers, and carry out a few.

Principle 5

KNOWING THAT MONEY IS NEVER THE REAL ISSUE

Money is essential to life but is not the purpose of life, but our money fears are usually the reason that we don't do what we want to do with our working lives. Money is not in itself a scarce resource; what may seem scarce are the necessary levels of creativity, self-belief, determination and courage. As we develop our inner strength and are willing to follow our heart, we will create and manifest opportunities to bring money into our lives. When we are willing to receive money and remove our blocks to it — our sense of guilt or unworthiness — we will bring money to us.

There is little likelihood that your life can become fully functioning with prosperity unless you have a positive and creative attitude toward money ... You may go into the day with the highest intention to walk in the light of Truth. But if you have not resolved the 'money enigma', you quickly lose your lofty awareness the moment you dip into your wallet.

ERIC BUTTERWORTH,
author of *Spiritual Economics*

To be truly successful in the work we were born to do, we need to carefully and honestly examine our relationship to money. If we don't, even our most beautiful, loving and creative ideas could flounder. The fear of not having enough money or financial insecurity is probably the biggest block we make to stop ourselves creating the work we were born to do. We have so much conditioning about money that we need to unravel.

Transforming Thought

Financial success is natural for you – you simply need to undo all your unhelpful conditioning about it.

EXERCISE

♦ Cast your mind back and remember your earliest memories about money. What meaning did your parents or guardians give to money? What did you decide about money as a result of that?

♦ When you think of money, what are the first ten words that come to mind?

♦ What are the three qualities you are least likely to associate with money?

♦ What are your deepest fears about money?

♦ What religious ideas do you have about money?

♦ If you don't have enough money, what does this prove in your mind?

♦ To what extent have you tied up your sense of identity with financial success?

Once we get clearer on the value we give money, we can choose how much of it is enough, and therefore what is a sufficiency for us. It may be that we can survive and thrive on less money and choose what is being called voluntary simplicity – less money, which gives more freedom in other areas.

Transforming Thought

No thoughts about money can stop you doing what you really feel called to.

HOW CAN WE EARN MONEY DOING WHAT WE LOVE?

1 Find what you love and what you are good at, what gives you joy

If you are in an uninspired place in your life, it is vital to find some things you enjoy and that excite you. Begin to do what you love and love what you do. Take it on as a project entitled 'Six months to refind my passion' and set a goal of trying at least one or two new things a week. Be determined to find a number of things you enjoy.

2 Practise and develop skills, confidence and abilities in your chosen area and just go for it

The issue need not be finding the time to start a new enterprise, but having the courage and willingness to make things work.

3 Capture all your money-making ideas

Have a notebook in which you capture all the ideas you have, and do your best to remember those you have had in the past. Keep answering the question, 'What would I love to be receiving money in return for being or doing?'

4 Be willing to learn and ask for feedback

If you have the courage to ask for feedback, and respond to both positive comments and constructive criticism, you will learn much that will help you to make even more of your gifts in your work.

5 Give your best, whatever the circumstances

Aim to give your best every time, right from the start, regardless of how much you may or may not be getting paid, whoever you are working for.

6 Have a strategy – start marketing, presenting and communicating who and what you are

Marketing is simply about letting people know who you are as well as what you do, and conveying the energy, the spirit of whatever you do. Everything you do on an outer level can convey this; brochures, letterheads, the actual product or the service itself can convey the essence of what you are about.

7   Be willing to receive

If we judge or dislike those with money, we'll limit how much we'll be open to receiving it. Be willing to receive money for easy and natural work, not just for hard work and struggle.

8   Learn to deal with all the resistance you encounter

As we choose to return to our natural state, our conditioning will be stimulated and we may experience fear, anger or guilt. We need to acknowledge these emotions whilst recognizing that they needn't stop us.

9   Be in the flow of money

Practise being in the flow and deriving as much pleasure from earning and receiving money as you do from spending and giving money. Practise giving money away too.

10   Be willing to start asking for and charging money

Many of us think we have to be perfect before we can start charging, but skills are only half the answer. Money is an exchange of energy, not just expertise.

Meditation

'I am willing to give up my confusion about money, and to accept that money is never really the issue. I wish to discover the self-esteem to ask for and receive the money that I need. I ask for the confidence to know that I will never go without, and that what life wants, life supports. Help me to know that money is an abundant resource.'

MONEY, FLOW AND EXCHANGE

There is no lack of actual money in the world, but there is a lack of will, of purpose, of courage, of vision and inspiration. And yet these qualities are within all of us, waiting to be drawn out. We worry about having enough money, when the key to having the money we want lies in finding the gifts and qualities that are in abundance inside us. When we have unlocked these gifts, the money we want will flow easily to and through us. Most of us dream of having fortune, but forget that we are a fortune in ourselves.

Affirmation

'Financial abundance will come to me through easily, lovingly, generously and joyfully giving and sharing my unique gifts. Abundance is in me, not in money.'

We all have our own natural and unique energy, a presence; we may need to develop it, but it is already there. Trust it: shine and you will be irresistible! Discover that the more you give of yourself freely in service, the more you are given to give. Give for the joy of giving.

EXERCISE

♦ When you say to yourself, 'If only I had money I would . . .', what difference do you believe it would make? What do you think, or tell yourself, you would do if you had more money?

♦ Be honest with yourself. Is it a lack of money that is *really* stopping you having what you want?

♦ Think about your own uniqueness. There is no one else like you. Write down any resistance and unhelpful beliefs you have about this idea.

♦ Identify your unique talents and the way that you do things well and beautifully; become aware of your niche.

♦ How can you *raise your energy* and bring more of your unique being into your work?

♦ Start doing and being what you want right now, with the money you have right now.

MISUNDERSTANDING THE VALUE OF OUR OWN GOODS AND SERVICES

We will receive money in direct proportion to what we are willing to give and what we are willing to receive. The more we choose to become a contributor, a giver, the more we become a magnet. The law of success is service and exchange.

Because we undervalue our abilities, lack self-esteem or feel fear, we can under-price what we do. We are sometimes unable to understand objectively what others are willing to pay. Other blocks to asking for what we are worth or what we want may include the following:

♦ not being clear about what we want

♦ not asking the right person

♦ guilt

Our sense of guilt is often an enormous block. It may show up as unworthiness, self-denial, judgement and criticism of those with money, self-sabotage or losing money. Many of us think that the creative power behind all life wants us to suffer and to do without. But we were not put on this earth to feel guilt. We must begin to feel really innocent about money, to know that we are innocent if we want money or if we have as much as we want, and to accept that our having money does not deprive others. We are entitled to exchange our gifts and skills for money. In the work we were born to do, money is a by-product of doing what we love, which is living the purpose we are here to fulfil.

Three Simple Ways to Implement Principle 5

* Let satisfaction, not money or recognition, be the measure of your success today.

* Give some money away today to someone whose need is greater than yours, and be present to notice their reaction, and your own reaction.

* Write down all the reasons you think you are worth a pay increase or putting your prices up. If you can't think of many, work out what *would* make you worth one.

Principle 6

WORKING ON PURPOSE

We find our purpose when we find and follow our inner knowing to discover and work at what we love. In so doing we channel our life energy into creating what matters most to us, rather than avoiding what we fear. Being on purpose will offer us many opportunities to move through doubt, obstacles and fear to a greater awareness of our true spirit.

It is better to follow your own life's mission (dharma), however imperfectly, than to assume the life mission of another person, however successfully.

When we find and follow our true purpose we will feel as if we are fully alive, rather than living a half-life. We will heal old hurts. We will feel whole and experience the greatest joy of all – living the life we were born to live and a deep fit between who we are and what we do. When we find our true purpose and vocation we will find that our gifts and talents intersect with the needs of the world and our fellow beings. This is why our true purpose is a gift to others too, and being on purpose is a win/win situation.

HOW DO WE DISCOVER OR REMEMBER OUR PURPOSE?

Purpose is unique for each one of us subject to where we are emotionally or financially in our lives. Each of us has something that our spirit is calling us to do, which will take us beyond our current perceived limitations.

Transforming Thought

Your purpose is to create more of what is precious to you and matters most in your life.

Start by knowing that your purpose is already within you, in the software of your consciousness, in your heart and soul. Most of us only discover our purpose later in life, after some wrong turns, although some people know theirs clearly from the beginning.

The bad news is that no one can tell you what your purpose is, although many – parents, teachers, religious leaders, politicians or employers – may have tried. They may have told you in the past, or you may still be waiting for them to tell you. But your true purpose is a calling and choice based on an inner feeling of rightness, of integrity and truth to yourself. Purpose is about having things to really live *for* in your work, giving your days and months a direction of your choice.

EXERCISE

♦ Are you on purpose? Ask yourself, 'Does this feel true for me?' and answer honestly.

♦ In simple terms, write a short statement about your life purpose. It doesn't have to state precisely where you are in your life, but it should feel true and convey the direction in which you are headed. Purpose can be the compass by which we guide our lives.

OUR SOUL'S PURPOSE

The truth is that each of us has come with particular gifts, qualities and talents to give, and particular things to heal in this life. Each of us is called to be and do something in life that only we can do in our unique way, and so we each have a vocation. Purpose is the daily and hourly living of our individual truth. It is for us to discover our purpose individually by listening to our own inner selves, our own hearts and bodies, through intuition.

EXERCISE

Try to answer the following questions as truthfully as you can.

♦ What is my life really about and what do I want it to be about?

♦ What gives me the experience of joy?

♦ What have I always longed to be/do?

♦ If I found I only had six months to live, how would I choose to spend them?

♦ When have I previously felt most purposeful in my life?

♦ Who do I know that seems to live a life of integrity and purpose?

♦ If I were to be clear about my purpose, it would be to . . .?

♦ Who annoys me most because they seem to have such a wonderful life?

♦ What does God/the creator want for me?

♦ What am I *for* in my life?

It can take some courage to be on purpose and to decide to create work based on being authentic and true to yourself.

Meditation

'Give me the courage to love and shine in a world that values fear and hiding. Give me the strength to overcome the obstacles I have created which block my awareness of my innate ability and beauty. I want to discover what will make my heart sing.'

REALIZING OUR WHOLE NATURE

The blocks to a purposeful life may seem to be outside us – money (as we saw in Principle 5), the economy, lack of resources or support – but mostly they are actually within us, in our own mind. On a deep level we may be scared stiff of our purpose. We may fear failure and embarrassment; we may even fear success and the size of our purpose. However, life never gives us a sense of purpose without also giving us the resources, guidance and support we need to see it through.

Living our purpose is about being willing to receive more and more gifts and to share them, and to re-own those gifts we may have thrown away out of fear when younger. It invites us to become whole and powerful again.

Affirmation

'I am committed to finding my life's purpose.'

Many of us spend our lives waiting to be discovered! Purpose calls us to rediscover ourselves, not wait for someone else to do it for us. It calls us to choose to bring out the best of ourselves for our own benefit and the benefit of others, to win back our heart and share what is precious. The irony is that it seems we would often rather live in pain and sorrow than swap that state for liberation – we are strange beings!

That is not to say that the path to the work we were born to do is without its own troubles. Travelling on it can sometimes be confusing as we may suddenly hit some resistance that has been buried just out of our awareness. We may need to attend to some of these buried and hidden parts of ourselves, known as our shadow.

FINDING THE COURAGE TO BE ON PURPOSE

Choosing to commit to answering our call to purpose may take us to all sorts of emotional places within ourselves where we may encounter joy and fear, insight and desperation, exuberance and poverty. This is because as we answer our call to purpose, we may need to do a certain amount of emotional, mental and spiritual spring-cleaning. Experiences and feelings that we buried away, and have spent much of our life and energy keeping buried, will resurface to be examined, felt and healed.

EXERCISE

♦ Be honest with yourself; what are the situations and experiences you spend most time and energy simply trying to avoid? Think for a moment about what it is you *least* want to experience in life; is it pain, failure, poverty, rejection, loneliness, feeling that life is meaningless, conflict, feeling lost, getting something wrong, looking stupid, disappointment – or a combination of these, or something else? Write them down.

♦ How do these feelings and this avoidance affect the quality of your life? How does this behaviour relate to your sense of purpose?

The truth is that most of us live an 'avoiding' rather than 'creating' purpose.

PURPOSE CALLS US TO COMMITMENT

We are often reluctant to answer and follow the call to our purpose, because we know that doing so may lead to big inner and outer change in our work. However, once we are clear about our purpose and don't resist it (which of course we probably will!), we can arrange events around it and, a little like iron filings around a magnet, our life will form around it too. When we say yes to purpose, there may be a short-term disruption as our life is re-arranged to be truer to and more supportive of our purpose.

Transforming Thought

Life moves to support your positive purpose. When you search for and remove the blocks to following your purpose, life will begin to do the rest.

Changing the direction and purpose of our life involves making a decision and a commitment and re-committing ourselves regularly, perhaps every day, as we face new challenges. Through commitment, we focus the whole power of our mind on a positive outcome, and are able to dissolve our doubts and fears as we continue to commit. As we keep committing, awareness of our vocation and calling will keep evolving.

Commitment is an ongoing process. It is easier to commit when things are going well, but we also need to commit when we are on our knees, when things are tough and when we *don't want to*. To commit means to keep giving and receiving continuously, not out of sacrifice, but out of choice. By choosing to commit, we will burn through layer after layer of resistance.

Three Simple Ways to Implement Principle 6

* If today were the last day of your life, how would you treat people? Do it anyway.

* Choose to be as authentic as you can be today.

* Make 'successes and things to be proud of' agenda items at your meetings or in your journal.

INTEGRITY, AUTHENTICITY AND THE RETURN TO WHOLENESS

We have buried much of our energy and hidden many of our qualities, gifts and talents deep in our mind because we were scared and felt they weren't approved of; and now we see them only in other people. We judge and fight our shadows by judging and fighting other people. We are on a journey of regaining our inner power by integrating these buried and split-off parts of ourselves.

Our spirit requires no approval or validation, for it knows no fear; it is only our roles, self-concepts and personalities based on fear that require approval.

When opposites no longer damage each other,
Both are benefited through the attainment of Tao ...
Therefore, the wise identifies opposites as one,
And sets an example for the world.

TAO TE CHING,
Taoist Scripture

Each of us is a diamond with many facets and flaws, some obvious and others hidden. Wholeness and authenticity are about beginning to unite our many fragmented aspects, for discovering our wholeness will return us to the awareness of our real nature, which lies at the heart of the work we were born to do. As we move towards wholeness, we may at times feel torn apart. This is because when we move forward, towards our hearts' desires, there can be forces within us that want to go back, stay put or sabotage our efforts. These forces are our shadows.

Meditation

'I ask for the strength to look at my shadows – those aspects of myself that I have judged and felt ashamed of. I ask for the power to accept what I have judged to be unacceptable, to become more authentic and to have greater integrity.'

WHAT ARE OUR SHADOWS?

Our shadows can be found beneath the niceties of our social roles. Our shadows are those parts of ourselves that we don't like, and which stop us being really happy, truly intimate or successful. They are the sum of all those aspects of ourselves that we have denied, devalued or disowned.

Our shadows may cause us discomfort or distress, so we

look for others to blame for how we feel. We take what we don't like about our characters and either condemn ourselves for it, or see it outside us, using the mechanism of projection to find in others what we have denied in ourselves. This means that the easiest way to identify what we have turned into our own dark shadows is to look out for what we can't stand in other people.

EXERCISE

- Who irritates you the most? What qualities about them most irritate you?

- To be accused of which quality most hurts and upsets you? For example, do you particularly resent being called selfish, insensitive, angry or uncaring?

- What are you most ashamed of being or doing?

- Who do you most hate at or through work?

- What quality would you deny is in you, which you can see clearly in other people?

As you answer these questions, you will begin to get greater insights into your personal shadows. We often fear that if people could see our shadows, they would recoil in horror and we'd be rejected. However, our shadows do not make us bad people, although they can perpetuate the belief that we are bad, which is unhelpful for our sense of self-worth and our efforts to succeed.

Transforming Thought

Each person to whom you have a strong reaction – negative or positive – is helping you to reclaim the buried treasure of your heart and mind.

We have light shadows as well as dark shadows. We may give away our power to our idols as well as to our enemies; for just as we give our nastiness to our enemies, so we may also give away much of our light, goodness, love, hope and spirit to our personal saviours or spiritual teachers.

EXERCISE

Here are some good exercises for applying Principle 7 to both our light and dark shadows.

♦ Identify your shadows of light. Who do you most admire, or even worship, and respect in or through work, but feel that you could never be like? Why could you never be like them? What changes would need to occur?

♦ Pick someone on a weekly basis who really pushes your buttons and place your judgements aside as much as you can. Talk to them and get to know them, recognizing that their offensive behaviour is simply a part of you that you don't like. See if you can accept or even like them.

♦ When you feel out of integrity, ask yourself 'If I were being authentic in this situation, what would I do or say?' Stay with that thought and see if it is appropriate to act on it.

Affirmation

'I am authentic in my work. I can create success and keep my integrity.

WHAT DO YOU REALLY THINK ABOUT DOING WHAT YOU LOVE?

The reality is that we are rather attached to these shadow selves, however awful they may be or whatever problems they cause us. We have trouble letting them go because to do so might mean change and even greater success.

Although consciously we all want to be fulfilled, happy and abundant in our work, we may well judge those who are already doing what they love.

EXERCISE

Think about your responses to the following questions:

♦ What is your opinion of happy and successful people?

♦ What do you think about people who have downshifted, or who have done what *they* wanted in life, dropped out or broken the rules of convention?

♦ What do you think of people who don't struggle or work long hours, and are self-determining, not motivated by fear?

If you have any strong negative feelings in response to any of these questions, be aware that these people may represent yet another part of your shadow self. If you judge them harshly, it is going to be a lot harder for you to develop their free-spirited qualities for yourself. If you don't like the way they are, you won't want to become like them and ultimately you won't share their contentment. You will need to make peace with those qualities before you can integrate them in your work.

Transforming Thought

You can safely integrate aspects of yourself that you have repressed.

HOW CAN WE INTEGRATE THESE DENIED PARTS OF US AND RECLAIM OUR POWER?

We can reclaim our power by joining – creating a connection – with those we are projecting onto or judging, seeing through to the divine core we all share. Some people call this hugging a monster, or feeling the fear and doing it anyway. When we hug a monster, we actually get to integrate the power that we have been splitting off from ourselves: we become stronger and truly whole. Here are some steps to achieve this:

♦ Be willing to acknowledge and simply be aware of your discomfort, judgements or thoughts of criticism or attack on other people.

♦ Be willing to say, 'Oops, yes, I do that too', and without guilt or judgement simply accept your behaviour, forgive both yourself and the other person and let go of your hostility. You will automatically feel a release, a lightness and an integration.

♦ Communicate with that person if you can. Transformational communication is achieved through simply naming how you are feeling, without blame. Then be willing to listen to the other person without defence or prejudice, which is often a real challenge. Don't even respond to start with, simply listen and breathe.

♦ Draw images or intend to have dreams about this shadow side and ask for integration through these processes.

♦ Close your eyes and imagine that in each hand you have what seem to be opposites and conflicting poles, for example good and bad, love and hate, judgement and acceptance, greed and selflessness, sensitivity and insensitivity. Visualize those energies, one in each hand, and then see, sense or feel them merging together. Bring your hands together and see a merging, a joining and an integration into a new strong whole. When we integrate opposites there is real power, because when parts of our mind are united and start to move in the same direction, our true creative power is increased.

♦ Be willing to see your innocence and the innocence of the other person in their actions. You cannot do that with your vision alone. You will need to call on the help of some greater power – whether you call it God, Buddha, the Holy Spirit, Love, Truth or whatever doesn't really matter. The key is simply to be willing to see with the vision of a force that can penetrate beyond appearances.

As we become more comfortable with the opposing forces within us, we will develop a greater level of inner power, of authenticity and the ability to contribute on a greater level. Once we have that power back, we can put it into creating the work we were born to do.

Three Simple Ways to Implement Principle 7

* Apologize to someone you've been harsh with, without justifying or putting yourself down.

* Think of somebody you are angry with and resentful of in your work sphere. Close your eyes and send them, and yourself, forgiveness. Wish them well.

* Notice who you are most angry with or irritated by in your working sphere. Ask yourself, 'What are the qualities I most dislike about this person?' List them on a piece (or pieces!) of paper. Recognize that those qualities are the ones you most dislike, or have most hidden, in yourself. Accept and become more comfortable with the qualities in yourself. Then see how *they* change!

Principle 8

CONTRIBUTION AND THE DISCOVERY OF MEANINGFUL WORK

Our greatest joy lies in finding our gifts and using them to enhance the lives of others. Knowing that all our lives weave together and that we are intrinsically valuable and connected makes our work meaningful. As we find <u>our</u> destiny, we help others find theirs. We can choose the kind of contribution we want to make and consciously discover the joy of giving and making a difference.

Consciously or unconsciously, every one of us does render some service or other. If we cultivate the habit of doing this service deliberately, our desire to serve will steadily grow stronger, and will make not only for our own happiness, but that of the world at large.

INDIRA PRIYADARSHINI GANDHI (1917–1984),
Prime Minister of India

What makes much work truly meaningful is the contribution it makes to our own life and the lives of those we work with and whose lives we touch. Although we live in a culture that seems to devote so much time and attention to communications of all sorts – telephone, fax, e-mail, letters, television, radio, advertising and marketing – there is still such loneliness in the world and a pervading sense of isolation. We can be surrounded by people at work or socially and still feel disconnected. What many of us seek is a quality of connection and contribution within our work and within our lives as a whole.

In truth, our lives are so interwoven that it is impossible for them *not* to have made an impact and contribution to thousands of other lives. Whether we are aware of it or not, and whether we feel a connection with society or not, our lives have already made a difference to the lives of incredible numbers of people – at work, at home, in the shops, on the street – virtually anyone with whom we have come into contact. If we had the opportunity to see the world as it would be if we hadn't been born, we would feel very differently, realizing how our current lives touch others in ways that we never even know about.

We never can and never will know just what contribution we do make, but what we do have power over is our *intention*, the contribution we intend and want to make.

Meditation

'I ask to be shown how to find the contribution I most truly want to make, and to share the best that is in me, knowing that my gifts are strengthened by sharing. Let me also learn how to help others without sacrificing myself.'

WORK, COMPASSION AND CONTRIBUTION

When we say we want meaningful and purposeful work or that we want to make a difference, what we actually mean, whether we are conscious of it or not, is that we want to serve and contribute. A great starting point for discovering the work you were born to do is to ask your heart to allow its natural compassion to suggest and guide you to creative and even joyful ways of serving this interconnected family of ours.

Transforming Thought

All your true gifts are strengthened by sharing and extending them.

Compassion arises when we realize that as human beings we all have similar experiences – we all have hopes and disappointments, pain and joy, loneliness and friendship. Compassion is choosing not to judge ourselves or others for the mistakes we have made, and to soften rather than harden our hearts. It cannot be forced or demanded, but comes naturally from the gradual understanding that what we do for others we are actually doing to and for ourselves.

EXERCISE

Think about your answers to the following questions.

- Who, either individuals or a group of people, do I feel particular compassion for?

- To relieve which human suffering do I feel the strongest call?

- Which unmet human aspirations would I most like to help people fulfil?

- Where does my motivation to serve come from – guilt, love, or a combination of the two?

- Why does the idea of serving and contributing *not* appeal to me?

True contribution requires no sacrifice, but follows from our compassion and draws upon our strengths, aptitudes, joy, interests, inspiration and passion. True contribution will energize us and help us to feel that we have arrived home in our heart.

Affirmation

'The more I give of myself, the more I have to give.'

GENUINE SERVICE

The work we were born to do is about responding to our inner call to serve. We will live very rich and full lives when we seek to contribute to the lives of others through our work. The two actually can – and indeed must – go beautifully together. Each of us has a generous spirit and a desire to give, and our work can become a major vehicle for our giving.

Any job can be carried out as an act of service, although we have tended to think that we either serve *or* go into business and commerce. But we can serve and be commercial; in fact, the most likely way we will be commercially successful will be by serving. Service is not only a luxury to be indulged when we are already successful; it is the path to true success.

Genuine service is the ability to focus on the needs of others without sacrificing our own needs, and to be willing to get under other people's skins in order to understand them and give them what they need.

EXERCISE

◆ Ask the magic questions:
  What do other people need or want?
  How can I help?
  How can I create a living helping others get what they want?
  How can I succeed by helping others to succeed?

◆ Think of some creative ways that you can make a contribution to the lives of others; for example, by sharing a book or a quotation, volunteering time or skills, making donations.

Service is one of the greatest ways to restore that awareness that we are already a divine being: we are not here to contact our Higher Self, but to *become* it.

GIVING AND RECEIVING

Service means getting into the flow of giving and receiving, which are two sides of the same coin. Giving and receiving are different manifestations of the same universal energy – spirit or love. No one can take away from us what we have given. True giving – from one heart to another – dissolves the emotional distance between ourselves and others and lessens the feeling of loneliness and separation. What we give is ultimately what we *get back*, and what we give is what we value and what we strengthen.

However, most of the giving we have experienced in our lives is *conditional*, by which I mean that it is giving for a purpose, and that purpose is to get something back in return. The trick is to learn to give more without wanting anything back, because when we expect something in return, we become attached to results. When we are attached, we block the flow, and less happens. Paradoxically, when we are not attached and do not expect a result, we will receive in vast quantities.

So why do we withhold? What do we think we gain from holding back on truly giving the best of ourselves?

EXERCISE

♦ Why do *you* withhold the best of yourself in your work and your life?

♦ What benefit do you think this defence gives you?

♦ What are you willing to give now?

WHAT CAN WE GIVE?

It is important to remember that the real value of our contribution often lies not so much in our actions or in hard work, but in our very being and presence. We can get so caught up in our conditioning – that work is all about doing – that we forget that our physical, emotional and spiritual presence can have great comfort and real power. In the workplace, for example, we can contribute in a simple and powerful way by:

♦ being centred, grounded and peaceful when others are flapping

♦ listening and accepting

♦ appreciating, valuing and enjoying people

♦ being enthusiastic

♦ looking for the good in every situation

♦ simply wishing people well and encouraging them

Each of us has the power to *feed* other people, and by that I don't mean with loaves and fishes, but with what we choose our life to be about, what we choose to spread, and what we choose to stand for. It is our arrogance that says we have nothing to offer. Our gifts and our self-worth are two different issues, and lack of self-worth will blind us to what we can have and can give.

Transforming Thought

You make a difference wherever you are and whatever you do, because of *who* you are.

We all have a valuable contribution to make, although we may need to address our sense of self-worth to realize this. Creating meaningful work will probably entail us changing our attitude or the actual work we do in some way, as we will see in Principle 9.

Three Simple Ways to Implement Principle 8

* Take an hour or two with colleagues to help in the community.

* Encourage colleagues and appreciate them.

* Do an anonymous and random act of kindness for someone through your work.

Principle 9

WELCOMING TRANSFORMATION AND CHANGE

Within each of us there lies the power to transform both our circumstances and, most importantly, our perceptions. As we set our intention to live more fully and authentically and move in that direction by making decisions and taking action, life will unfold for us. We can then begin to work in partnership with the realm of spirit to dissolve our fear-based perceptions and discover the truth of love and creativity.

No one is comfortable when they begin the journey from the known to the unknown, but we can be comforted by the knowledge that the summit is not really new. We are not leaving home; we are coming home. We used to live on this higher ground a long time ago — we are simply reclaiming it. It beckons us to return.

LANCE SECRETAN,
Management consultant and author of
Reclaiming Higher Ground

Change is integral to the work we were born to do, in which there is only one true direction of change and that is towards our authentic and true Self, gradually leaving behind fear, roles, limitations and compensations to embrace love, creativity, integrity, wholeness and our own nature as spirit.

Transforming Thought

Our fear of change, of being born into our true selves, is probably our greatest fear. We would rather have all our problems than be free.

FEAR OF CHANGE

We may fear change and resist it by holding on to whatever we think we've achieved and accumulated, believing this is probably about as good as it gets. However, we won't be open to the success on offer *now* if we are still holding on to *then*.

EXERCISE

Here are some questions to answer:

♦ How much are you still holding on to the good old days?

How much are you still comparing what was with what is? Close your eyes and give thanks for those experiences, the people you've known and worked with, the closeness and team spirit you had then. Be grateful and then let go of them.

♦ What are some of your insecurities? (Include the ones that make no logical sense, but can *feel* very real.) Are you going to let them stop you instigating change?

♦ If you had no sense of fear or guilt, and felt free to choose, in what direction would you really want to move?

♦ Have you thought about the best and most wonderful things you could experience as a result of the change(s) you are considering making?

Meditation

'Let me face the changes I choose, and the changes thrust upon me, with courage and optimism. Let me be willing to face feelings of loss and grief if necessary, and to find the power to change my perceptions as well as my circumstances. Help me to know that the unknown is full of wonderful things.'

Letting go is like shedding a skin and a rebirth – sometimes a painful process but essential for growth. When we truly let go of our emotional attachment to a thing or person, one of two wonderful things happens:

We still have what we used to have, but with a
greater level of freedom and abundance,
or
We don't have what we used to have any more –
although we still have all the memories, benefits or
gifts of it – but something new and even better
moves into our life to take its place.

Affirmation

'I am willing to make positive changes in my life.'

OUR SENSE OF IDENTITY AND
THE DESIRE FOR SECURITY

The conscious desire to feel secure is natural and important.
The only question is, 'From where or whom do we think our
sense of security derives?' Our ability to surf the waves of
change hinges on our sense of identity – who we think we are.
The more we identify ourselves with externals, achievements
and everything impermanent, the more we tend to cling. We
can put a lot of energy into trying to maintain and defend our
identity, leaving us little energy to be creative.

In these times, the bad news is that there is no security in
any job, indeed in any line of work. The good news is that real
security lies deep within us, because our spirit, creativity,
determination and ability to change are truly limitless. The
source, of which we are a part, is forever flowing, although the
forms in which it manifests are constantly changing. True
security resides in the creativity within us, and awareness of
this will contribute to our feeling of stability, for creativity
is never more than a thought away, in all places and at all
times. True security means knowing that we have the creative
imagination to always earn a living.

EXERCISE

♦ Think back to some of the most challenging times in your life, even the times when you felt floored and wanted to give up. In retrospect, how have you grown in consciousness into a bigger, wiser, more compassionate person?

♦ Cast your mind back over some of the major changes you have already experienced in your life, perhaps involving careers and work, relationships or bereavements. Pick a specific one. What resources got you through? How were you strengthened by this change?

It is good to remind ourselves that whilst change is likely to move us away from what is known and comfortable, all that is now known and comfortable once wasn't. We have already changed so many times!

Transforming Thought

The unknown is overflowing with the new, the curious and the exciting – all waiting for you!

DECIDING TO CHANGE

Conscious decisions to change are some of the most important ways to find the work we were born to do. You can decide to liberate yourself to change.

1 Listen to your heart and intuition, and act on it – decide on the direction, or essence, of your change

Your first job is simple and powerful – be willing to change.

2 Baby steps

Every big success started from a small beginning. You can choose to make small changes right now, and start where it is easiest, to build up your confidence.

3 The first steps in faith

You are called to let go of what you are familiar with and what is known, and to take your first steps in faith. When you refuse to cling to the past, you will always be given more.

4 Explore – you really don't know

Get more and more comfortable with the idea that you don't know for sure what changing may involve or lead to. Be happier with, 'I don't know, but I can discover/be shown.'

5 Commitment and trust – doing whatever it takes

As long as you commit and refuse to cling to old ways and old patterns, you will be rewarded with success, and by a life that is supported by the work you love.

6 Relinquish some control and let life unfold

When you are willing to let go of control, amazing events can manifest. You can determine how you will *respond* to whatever circumstances you find yourself in.

7 Get love and support

If you are a tough-it-out-on-your-own kind of person, be willing to start reaching out and asking for help and support on inner and outer levels.

8   Be willing to have it be as good as possible – now and always

Remember to live in the here and now, where life can actively support you.

9   Put attention on that which is changeless

Behind all changing appearances is a changeless spirit. Take time to focus on the source of all that changes, which itself doesn't change.

PERMISSION TO TAKE A BREAK

We should all give ourselves permission simply to take a break, a sabbatical if possible or at least a few days. We need opportunities to take stock and have some head and heart space to think and feel about who we are and where we are. You may have dismissed the idea of taking a break as an impossible luxury, but is it really?

EXERCISE

Consider the following questions:

♦ What are your fearful thoughts about taking a break?

♦ What is the *best* that could happen from taking a break?

Take time to sit down and think and brainstorm how you could do it. Calculate your finances and see how much you have and would need. Simply be with the question, 'How *could* I take a career break?' Notice what thoughts come to you.

MAKING THE TRANSITION

Taking a career break or making the transition from, say, a salary to self-employment, or starting a new project, may or may not mean that we have to take a temporary financial drop. We need to keep remembering that if we earned money once, we can do so again; and, even if we haven't earned much yet, if we set store by our natural prosperity – our innate abilities – we can be confident that we will earn money in the future.

It is quite possible that the work we were born to do will be a portfolio – not a single job or place of work, but work with several strands to it, each allowing us to express different aspects of ourselves, with some providing us with financial means whilst others are where our heart truly lies. Portfolio working is a legitimate way of working that is growing hugely in popularity.

Interestingly, getting by on less money for a while actually stimulates creativity, and often leads to increased gratitude for what we already have. As we become happier in our work, we will need less financial compensation because the work becomes its own reward. Money becomes an extra reward.

Three Simple Ways to Implement Principle 9

* Review three of the biggest changes in your life and recognize how you have grown through them.

* Take two small steps today to improve the quality of your working life.

* Write down three areas in which you feel trapped. For each one, come up with three possible creative and original solutions.

Principle 10

THE INSPIRATION
TO CREATE

Creativity means either infusing our work with our own uniqueness or bringing ideas from the realms of our mind and imagination into physical reality. Creativity is natural to us and, as we remove the blocks we have erected to our naturalness, we will find ourselves becoming channels for creative ideas and energy and becoming co-creators with life. Creative action is the way we turn inspiration into action and achievements.

The delusive idea that men merely toil and work for the sake of preserving their bodies and procuring for themselves bread, houses and clothes is degrading, and not to be encouraged. The true origin of man's activity and creativeness lies in his increasing impulse to embody outside of himself the divine and spiritual element within him.

FRIEDRICH FROBEL (1782–1852),
German educator and founder of Kindergarten

Creativity lies at the heart of the work we were born to do and exists within each one of us right at this moment. We all have the power to create the work we were born to do. Nothing wonderful ever happened that wasn't first shaped by an idea in a creative mind, which includes *your* life and *your* mind. Creativity is a way of saying, 'I am alive, I am here and expressing life.'

There are two forms of creativity. Firstly there is what we might call small 'c' creativity, which is about acting with originality, putting our unique talents and energy into our work whatever it is – the report we are writing, the presentation we have to give, the way we manage our work.

Then there is big 'C' Creativity. This is concerned with our God-given ability to bring into existence something that doesn't currently exist, to see and create our own future. It is in our nature to imagine and shape our world, and when we do so in the spirit of love and compassion our creativity can literally bring heaven to earth. We can become more conscious of the creative process running through nature as a whole, and bring the ideas in our own creative imaginations into reality. We can create the work we were born to do if it doesn't already exist.

OUR RESISTANCE TO CREATIVITY

Culturally, creativity is often marginalized, bracketed as 'the Arts' and perhaps even seen as irrelevant or harmful to our everyday working lives. Because many of us have rarely been encouraged to think of ourselves as creative, perhaps the biggest challenge we face is the core belief that we have no creative ability.

Remember that beliefs are not facts. Belief in our lack of creativity simply hide our awareness of and access to our creative energy; they don't cancel out the energy itself. Once we acknowledge our unhelpful thoughts, attend to our feelings about them and discard our core negative beliefs, our creative energy will be waiting for us like a fresh spring, waiting for us to plunge into it again.

Transforming Thought

You can never run out of creativity, although you may appear to. In time, you can dissolve all blocks to your creative awareness and energy.

Although it can take courage to take the plunge and follow a creative life, it's more painful to live a diminished or uncreative life. Courage means having the willingness to act though things might not turn out as expected, but most of all courage means the willingness to trust that, whatever appearances may indicate, life really is *for* us. Perhaps surprisingly, in the work we were born to do we can grow just as much through what appear to be failures as we can through seeming successes.

EXERCISE

◆ What do creativity and being creative mean to you?

♦ Why do you think life wouldn't support you in following your creative purpose?

♦ Write down your positive and negative responses to the following true statement:

'I [insert your name] am a gifted, talented and creative individual, and have access to the creative energy that has been available to every person that ever walked this planet. I can find, follow and discover ways of being creative and eventually supporting myself financially from my creative impulses and creative ideas.'

What do your responses tell you?

Meditation

'I am willing to understand just how creative I already am, that my world of experience is already my own creation. I am willing to release, layer by layer, my feelings of being a victim and to give up the blame I have used to hold myself back. I ask to be a co-creator with life, to bring into being the most amazing ideas that are in my heart and mind.'

REDISCOVER YOUR CREATIVITY

We are all artists in one fashion or another, although each one of us may have a different medium for our creativity and a different way of expressing it. It may be singing, writing, dancing, laughing, storytelling, reading, drawing, painting, solving problems, listening, being a parent, gardening, homemaking or flower arranging. There is an unlimited number of ways to be creative. You are already sitting on your own talent and gifts, so go exploring for them and determine not to give up looking for them.

Transforming Thought

You almost have an obligation to share your creative gifts and talents, in whatever form you have them. Your fulfilment will come from finding and sharing your creativity.

One way you can start to look for your creative gifts is to answer the question, 'What do I want to get fascinated by?' Remember that what we pay attention to, we start to become. By deciding to become fascinated by what you love and enjoy, by what you are touched, inspired and moved by, you will sow the seeds of the work you were born to do. But you won't reap a harvest of positiveness by sowing seeds of negativity, just as apple seeds don't produce oranges.

EXERCISE

♦ Take some time to be still, and ask yourself the question, 'If I were to put creativity, creative ideas and my creative power centre stage in my life, what might that look like?' Note the ideas and thoughts that come to you.

♦ Decide what you want to become fascinated by and what you would like to become an expert on. Start immersing yourself in that area and start an inner and outer discovery process.

♦ Try something new on a regular basis: go out (with a friend if that helps) to a salsa class, enrol on a course for creative writing, a martial art, film making, musical appreciation or whatever inspires you.

♦ What dreams have you had over the years, since childhood, that you have abandoned or forgotten?

♦ What is the boldest vision you have ever had for your life? Write it down even if it feels like a mad or arrogant fantasy.

Start being creative now! Take a creative risk every day. Put more of *you*, your originality, your love, fun, humour, whackiness, heart or care into whatever you do. Build up your creative muscle.

Affirmation

'I am open to inspiration in my work.'

Take some time to think about what you are going to make a long-term creative commitment to, not just in the early stages of your excitement, but when the initial glow has worn off. Settle on something that you will stick with during the power-struggle times, the dead times when you feel like you've lost it, when no one else cares and you wonder if you even care. Make a commitment to hang in there no matter how exciting, challenging, scared or successful you become. Committing to the work we were born to do is a life-time project that takes as long as it takes.

CREATING OUR OWN WORK

The most exciting creative act is to bring the work we were born to do into being – to take an idea from the realm of thought and imagination and make it truly happen in the physical world.

EXERCISE

Below is a brief action strategy for creating your own work:

◆ Ask yourself what else you could imagine yourself doing or being in work. What can you do to realize this dream? What regular action might you take? Have a vision in your mind's eye – something that touches your heart, excites and inspires you, and something that you know will help other people.

◆ Get clear on the essence, not the form, of the vision – what qualities do you want to give and share? Keep your inner and outer attention on this essence.

◆ Be willing to face any old hurts or self-doubts and to keep on going, however hard it may seem to get.

◆ Live the paradox of wanting to create your vision while at the same time letting go as much as possible of your emotional attachment to the outcome.

◆ Grow in your awareness that life is *for* you and that when you commit to your intentions, life orchestrates opportunities for the fulfilment of your intention, when your intention is based on love.

◆ Avoid linking creativity and the commercialization of your creativity too soon. Don't put too much pressure on your fledgling creativity. Allow time for your ideas and skills to take flight.

◆ Be patient with yourself. Over and over again people drop creative ideas that don't come to immediate fruition, not realizing that if they had stayed focused on their goal it would have eventually become real.

There is no one route to creating the work we were born to do – we make the path as we set out to walk it. It cannot be mapped

out in advance, but will unfold as we commit to living by our values and our principles. Then we move from a job to an adventure. And we can be sure that, whatever path we choose, through following our creativity we will blaze a trail for others, just as others have done for us.

Three Simple Ways to Implement Principle 10

* Take a creative risk today in work. Be original or whacky or set a creative idea in motion.

* Take or give a 'wellness day' – a day away from work feeling well and happy, so as to avoid a future illness. Refresh and recreate yourself.

* Listen to an inspiring tape on the way to work and notice how your day is different.

Principle 11

ABUNDANCE AND
INNER RICHNESS

Abundance is our natural state, a consciousness of the all-sufficiency of supply, where we are open to receiving and sharing the gifts of spirit, but which most of us have blocked through guilt and feelings of unworthiness. As we reclaim our own sense of self-worth, focus on the source – not the effects – and choose to put ourselves back in the flow of giving and receiving, we will release thoughts of lack and reclaim our abundance.

You may frustrate your potential. You may identify with that which is less than you can be. But within you now and always is the unborn possibility of a limitless experience of inner stability and outer treasure, and yours is the privilege of giving birth to it. And you will, if you can believe.

ERIC BUTTERWORTH,
author of *Spiritual Economics*

We can all live by a simple truth – the more we give and share, the more we will receive. True abundance is the willingness to keep on receiving and sharing the endless gifts of life. It dissolves our dual fears of giving and receiving. The supply side of spiritual abundance is never an issue; it is guaranteed and unlimited. Within us is our own source of incredible abundance, which can flow from us and through us. All we need to do is get out of its way. Unfortunately most of us have been conditioned to cut ourselves off from this supply of abundance.

EXERCISE

Let's consider some of our expectations about abundance:

♦ What are your images of abundance? For some it may be the horn of plenty, an ever-opening flower, the loaves and fishes miracle, nature. What are yours?

♦ What is your relationship to abundance? Do you believe in it, but think it is not for you? Do you think it doesn't exist; it is a cruel joke, an unattainable idea? Do you feel you don't know how to access it? Do you rely on the abundance of others?

♦ What was there an abundance of in your family of origin? For example, was there a limitless supply of love, money, fun, appreciation, support, criticism, worry, neurosis, debt?

♦ When you were young, at home or at school, was there something you felt there wasn't enough of? Time, money, opportunity, love? What did you decide about yourself and the world as a result of those thoughts?

♦ When and why did you decide it wasn't safe to receive in your life?

♦ Identify six areas of your life now where you experience a sense of lack (including a sense of emptiness or neediness). What do you think will fill these areas of lack? How successful have you been so far in removing this sense of lack?

We take lack and scarcity as a *fact*, and on a surface level we'd be mad not to. Just look around at all the evidence. Too few people do what they love for a living; there are hundreds if not thousands of applications for some jobs; perhaps two thirds of the world live in poverty; there is competition, battles and strife; firms go bankrupt all the time. This seems to be our reality.

Meditation

'I wish to know in my heart that scarcity, lack and competition are not reality. I am willing to shed my beliefs in scarcity and step into the abundance and plenty that is my true nature.'

Yet we get cause and effect the wrong way round. The circumstances I have just mentioned are not the cause of lack; they are the consequence of our belief in it. And because we believe in lack, we create and, most importantly, we experience lack.

> ### Transforming Thought
>
> Abundance already exists; the only limit to abundance is your willingness to be aware of and to receive it.

UNDOING BLOCKS TO ABUNDANCE IN WORK

Abundance is not about our circumstances, but about developing an awareness of existing inner prosperity. It is primarily a feeling. Abundance is not a miracle, but a natural principle, and like most other principles, it is experienced by identifying and removing the blocks that we have learned and created. These blocks can include the belief that:

- ♦ scarcity is our natural state

- ♦ we need to compete to survive

- ♦ we are not worthy of receiving

- ♦ we shouldn't take risks to discover what we enjoy

- ♦ true abundance means frightening changes

- ♦ other people or situations are to blame for our not experiencing abundance

- ♦ we need the details to be perfect before we can experience abundance

- ♦ only certain special people can be abundant

In truth we live in a world of unlimited potential and unlimited creative opportunity. New opportunity is an every moment reality, when we stop letting fear and lack cloud our vision. When we replace fear with excitement and willingness, our perception of any situation can transform it into abundance.

Affirmation

'I am willing to be abundant.'

EXERCISE

♦ What do you expect to experience as a result of finding and creating the work you were born to do? Joy, fulfilment, a sense of purpose ...? List your thoughts.

♦ Focus on where in your life you already experience some of these qualities, though maybe just in small quantities at the moment. Make the most of them now.

Transforming Thought

Abundance flows naturally as a result of your discovering and doing what you love, and from following your heart.

WHAT DO WE WANT MORE OF?

True prosperity is a mental and emotional state, a way of thinking and a level of consciousness. We can be incredibly wealthy, yet feel poor and scared, living in fear of losing what we have, or we can be materially poor and feel like a king or queen.

EXERCISE

Here are some strategies to bring about the experience of abundance in your work:

1 Intention

Hold the thought in your mind that you have decided to live abundantly. By holding the image of abundant living in your mind, your intention will start to manifest.

2 Be *for* not against

Whatever you don't want and are against, you actually give power to and help keep going. You get what you want by focusing on it and creating it.

3 Be thankful – focus on what is present, not on what is missing

Continue a daily gratitude diet.

4 Do what you love, and love what you do

Start choosing to do things in life and work that you enjoy.

5 Stretch – give more when it pinches, not less

We often say to ourselves, 'When I feel comfortable, *then* I'll be more abundant.' So when you feel inclined to hold back, try stretching *into* abundance.

6 Ask for abundance

When faced with a situation that seems difficult to resolve because of some issue of lack, try asking yourself an empowering question like, 'What would be an abundant solution to this situation?'

7 Remember that we are stewards, not owners

It is worth remembering that in 50 or 100 years everything that we are now so scared to lose will probably belong to someone else or won't exist any more. That should help you to stop holding on so tightly.

8 Be affluent

Be in the flow of abundance – the good things in life. To get the flow going, give something for free to someone who could really use it. It could be your time, energy or money.

9 Practise some luxury

Notice where you *make do*, then choose not to, but go for the best of whatever you can.

10 Practise the joy of receiving

Write this in big letters and keep it above your desk or dressing table – 'It is just as holy to receive as it is to give'! Go on a receiving spree!

11 Give for the Sheer Joy of Giving

Although work is not usually thought of as a place of natural generosity, let's practise giving for no other reward than the sheer joy of doing it. Practise small random acts of kindness.

12 Cultivate freedom in your work

Freedom in work may sound like a contradiction in terms, but it is not. A major quality of abundance is freedom, because true abundance contains no fear. When you truly choose to do what is in front of you, you begin to find freedom.

13 Know that everything you are looking for is inside

You are the presence of everything you are looking for, as *all* experiences are in your own mind. Abundance comes from within: you need do nothing, other than peel off the layers of conditioning.

14 Celebrate the successes of others

Learn to celebrate others' achievements. Experience sympathetic joy, which invites you to feel the joy of others not as an attack on you but as a gift.

15 Unlimited opportunities

Know that there are no limits to the opportunities available in life, and that you can find or create the niche that is right for you and not just take what isn't true for you.

True wealth is measured by what we have found in ourselves, shared and given in our lives, not just by how much we've accumulated. So let's now complete our journey by discovering the true meaning of success.

Three Simple Ways to Implement Principle 11

* Choose to give more willingly than is expected of you.
* Ask for something that you really want but have never asked for before in work.
* Receive something that you've been saying 'No' to.

Principle 12

EXPERIENCING THE TRUE
MEANING OF SUCCESS

Old ideas of success might be measured by what we achieve materially, but more importantly it is becoming aware of who we are in the process of discovering the work we were born to do. True success means finding our heart and soul and bringing them into whatever we do, whilst having the material and financial support we need. True success is not of this world, but is in the realm of spirit. It means knowing ourselves as children of our creator, as spirit.

What lies behind us and lies before us are small matters compared to what lies within us. And when we bring what is within out into the world, miracles happen.

HENRY DAVID THOREAU (1817–1862),
writer and social critic

You have already achieved great success simply by being willing to open your mind to so many new ideas. So, how does it feel to have come so far? And how can you take the next step towards really beginning to enjoy your success?

True success depends not on what we know, but what we do with what we know. It's about who we have come to be on this planet – how we discover our true power and innocence by gradually releasing guilt and fear. How big a leap are you willing to take? What have you come to give the world that would make you so happy, so thrilled, and probably so scared? Whatever it is, be sure that it is a great thing!

EXERCISE

♦ Think about and list all your options, at this moment, as you currently perceive them.

♦ Which one(s) most appeal to you and inspire you?

♦ If you don't have one that really appeals, make 'Discovering what really appeals to me' an ongoing project.

♦ Decide on six positive steps that you can take over the next 28 days to explore or create these options.

♦ Create an ideal 'everything is possible' type of work/job description for yourself. What would be ideal for you?

♦ On your epitaph, would you have been known for giving?

What message would you most like to have delivered to the world?

Meditation

'Let me understand that true success is knowing my true nature as a creative, spiritual being, free of guilt and fear. Give me the courage to see past all appearances and accept the wonderful truth about myself and all my fellow beings.'

Success in experiencing the work we were born to do is achieved through a process of daily decisions to practise the ideas we have talked about in this book. Many times every day we are offered opportunities to either step into new ways of working, living and being, or stay with or slip back into old familiar ways. That is the great news – the constant opportunities to choose abundance over lack, to choose love and creativity over fear, and to be authentic rather than play a role and please others.

Transforming Thought

True success is created not from conscious effort alone, but in partnership with our deepest, creative mind.

IN WHAT WAYS WILL THE WORK WE WERE BORN TO DO BE SUCCESSFUL?

Most of what we have come to know as success is what we believe we *should* want, and is largely concerned with our outer world and what we have achieved, bought and accumulated. The work we were born to do is concerned with realizing success, but in ways that may differ from our usual expectations.

EXERCISE

♦ First, have a look at what you believe you must do/achieve/have in order to *be successful*. What would success mean for you? Would it be, for example, no debts, no anger, a large house, fame and fortune? As usual, be as honest with yourself as you can.

♦ If you left out all mention of money, achievements and material possessions, how would you define success for yourself? For example, would your true measure of success be 'feeling on purpose in my life', 'feeling confident in my ability to handle the situations of my life as they arise', 'being in touch with my creativity and knowing that I am loved', 'stepping through my fears'…?

> Affirmation
>
> 'I am enough.'

12 FINAL STEPS

Here, in conclusion, are some simple guidelines for setting out today on the path to the work you were born to do.

EXERCISE

1 Trust your inner knowledge over your doubts

Banish your doubts and start developing that sense of certainty now! Put all your love, energy and resources into a single direction, and make a commitment to it.

2 Develop self-belief

Start small and celebrate all the little steps in your intended direction. Make the most of your small achievements and under-criticize yourself for any mistakes.

3 Stretch yourself a little every day and act on your inner knowledge

Choose to stretch out beyond your beliefs and perceived limits. On a daily basis, do something that will positively enhance your life, but which you may feel scared about. Try to do it with as little attachment as possible to the outcome.

4 Aim to demonstrate, not prove

Trying to create anything in life in order to prove something to someone implies underlying doubt, which is the basis of fear. You can't *prove* your value, but you can let value flow from you into all you do.

5 Integrate inner and outer success

Try to let go once and for all of the idea that inner and outer success are in conflict or incompatible, and realize instead that the two are totally interwoven – they need not be in conflict but should be in balance. Whilst you are on the path to discovering the work you were born to do, you will still need to feed, clothe and house yourself; you are not being asked to make sacrifices but to change your perceptions.

6 Decide what you will make more important than fear

Acknowledge each fearful thought as an opportunity to recognize that you have a choice – either to let fear rule and restrict your life, or to make something else more important.

7 Keep stepping through the biggest fear of all – the fear of happiness, joy and true success

It has been said that there is only one thing worse than not getting what we want, and that is getting what we want! Often our biggest fears are actually the *very things* we claim we want so much – happiness, joy, love, abundance and freedom! Be truly willing to put down your defences and let bounty in.

8 Resist the urge to sabotage

Sabotage shows up in many ways, from having a brilliant idea but not following it up, through to not accepting help from others. Self-sabotage has its roots in guilt or fear of loss. Know that you need not feel guilty about being successful and that ultimately you have much more to lose by sabotaging your own efforts than you have to gain.

9 Practise unattachment

To be unattached means to be genuinely without need. Try to create from a place of not needing, but wanting. True detachment means giving our all, not out of naïveté, but out of truth without knowing what the outcome will be.

10 Know that the ultimate success is not what you achieve, but becoming aware of who you are in the process

We are so trained and conditioned to believe that the purpose of life has something to do with our success in the world out there, and how much we get of it. What if the true purpose of life was simply to know ourselves, to know who we really are behind all the ideas of who we think we are, to know our own spiritual nature? Let your outer success be at the expanse of, not the expense of, your inner being.

11 Move forward in faith

Moving forward in faith means trusting in the universe and allowing yourself to go with the flow, relinquishing control. It is about working in partnership with the intangible, invisible and all-pervading energy behind the whole of creation. This is the force that helps us to manifest physically what we first believed in and only saw in our mind's eye.

12 Experience the joy and fulfilment of letting love be our guide

So much of our energy can go into getting people to like us, accept us, approve of us and not reject us. Realize that love is within you and that you can give love and encouragement to the very people you used to demand it from. Let your heart lead the way.

Whatever your life story so far, you already have greatness and genius within you; we all have the mind of the universe buried deep within us. We are God's great ideas.

Transforming Thought

True success is about knowing who you are in essence, your own heart and the inherent beauty of who you are.

Success is something not to obtain but to be and to remember: you will find success by giving and receiving love, peace, joy and abundance. Success is not about being in control but about being open and guided. It is not about winning, but about opening up to being your best Self, giving and receiving all, and opening a voice for spirit. Your natural success is a blessing to yourself and those around you.

Be bold – take your place centre stage in your own life, and know how blessed you are on the journey home to your heart.

Three Simple Ways to Implement Principle 12

* Celebrate yourself. Write down, for yourself, ten things that you are good at and that you contribute through your work.

* Ask for a miracle in the working life of someone you know who is facing challenges.

* Celebrate something that is not special but that has gone well.

The Sheffield College
Hillsborough LRC

Conclusion

As soon as your subconcious accepts any idea, it proceeds
to put into effect immediately ... Sometimes it seems to bring
about an immediate solution to your difficulties, but at
other times it may take days, weeks or longer ... *Its ways are
past finding out.*

DR JOSEPH MURPHY
Author of *The Power of Your Subconscious Mind*

The journey to creating the work we were born to do is not
always easy; it may involve some of the toughest and at the
same time scariest decisions we ever make. But we simply need
to remember that life is always on our side, and that we just
need to get out of our own way. All of our achievements will
come to us through a series of small steps, so keep moving a
pace at a time in the direction your heart calls you.

You are not alone in your quest to discover the work you
were born to do, and once you set your intention you will be
supported every step of the way. Be willing to open to new and
greater levels of love, friendship and support. And don't be
afraid to ask for what you need; there is always help available.

Most of all, have the courage to shine. The greatest gift you
have is who you are, your being; you are more wonderful than
any achievement.

Useful Addresses

Heart at Work support products and services

Heart at Work, founded by Nick Williams, aims to serve the needs of three key groups:

1. Individuals seeking career inspiration and guidance.

2. Individuals considering or already running their own small businesses, based on their passions.

3. Organisations in the public, private and voluntary sector who want to inspire the best from their staff.

· Heart at Work runs regular events around the UK, and we'll happily send you a programme, or look at our website.

· One-to-one coaching with Nick Williams or a skilled colleague

· We run an 8-week 'Heart at Work' programme to help you lay the foundations for your work and success

· We offer a free monthly e-newsletter with inspiration and ideas

· We offer a year-long 'Soul Power' e-mail coaching programme. Every week for 52 weeks you will receive e-mail coaching direct from Nick Williams to help you create unconditional success and the work you were born to do. This costs only £35 for a whole year.

Contact us for full information on how we can work with your company or conference, from a 60-minute presentation, to a year-long programme.

For information on these contact us at:

UK
Nick Williams
The Heart at Work
PO Box 2236
London W1A 5UA
tel: 07000-781922
e-mail: success@heartatwork.net
website: www.heartatwork.net

Alternatives (where Nick was director for many years)
St James's
197 Piccadilly
London W1J 9FF
tel: 020 7287 6711
e-mail: post@alternatives.org.uk
website: www.alternatives.org.uk

Partner organisations
around the globe:

USA
Barbara Winter
Winning Ways
PO Box 390412
Minneapolis
MN 55439
tel: 001 952 835 5647
e-mail:
babswinter@yahoo.com

SOUTH AFRICA
Helen Burton
Cape Town, South Africa
tel (cell phone): 00 27 21
(0)825777772
e-mail:
burton@intekom.co.za

IRELAND
Michael Daly
The Barnabas Project
152 Willow Park Drive
Glasnevin, Dublin 11
tel: 00 353 1 842 0544
e-mail:
barnabas@gofree.indigo.ie

NEW ZEALAND
Liz Constable
Life Coach
12 Hollywood Ave
Titirangi
Auckland
New Zealand
tel: 00 649 817 5189
e-mail:
goddess@planet.gen.nz

AUSTRALIA
Ian Hutchinson
Life by Design
Suite 19, 88 Helen Street
Lane Cove
NSW 2066
Australia
tel: 00 61 2 9420 8280
fax: 00 61 2 9418 7747
e-mail:
info@lifebydesign.com.au
website:
www.lifebydesign.com.au

Index